Skateboar

Legendary Tricks 2

Steve Badillo

Tricks and Photography
by Steve Badillo
unless otherwise noted

TRACKS

Tracks Publishing
San Diego, California

Skateboarding: Legendary Tricks 2
by Steve Badillo

Tracks Publishing
140 Brightwood Avenue
Chula Vista, CA 91910
619-476-7125
tracks@cox.net
www.trackspublishing.com

Copyright © 2010 by Doug Werner and Steve Badillo
10 9 8 7 6 5 4 3 2 1

The information contained in this book is based on material supplied to the Author and Tracks Publishing. While every effort has been made to ensure accuracy, and to attribute and credit all work, the Author and Tracks Publishing do not under any circumstances accept responsibility for any errors or omissions. Trademarked names are used in this book; however, instead of placing a trademark symbol beside every occurrence of a trademarked name, we state the trademarked names are used only in an editorial fashion and to the benefit of the trademark owner. No infringement of the trademark is intended. All images are owned by the Author or were obtained solely by the Author through private collections, or supplied courtesy of private collectors. With respect to the privacy of these individuals, all contributors and sources are credited with no association to possessions unless expressly requested otherwise.

Publisher's Cataloging-in-Publication

Badillo, Steve.
    Skateboarding : legendary tricks 2 / Steve Badillo ;
tricks and photography by Steve Badillo unless otherwise
noted.
    p. cm.
    Includes bibliographical references and index.
    LCCN 2009942077
    ISBN-13: 978-1-884654-35-0
    ISBN-10: 1-884654-35-5

    1. Skateboarding. 2. Skateboarding--Pictorial works.
I. Title. II. Title: Legendary tricks 2.

GV859.8.B335 2010   796.22
                             QBI09-600225

This book is dedicated to longtime NYC pioneer skateboarder and skatepark designer Andy Kessler. Thanks for taking skateboarding in the right direction. Making something from nothing. You will be missed. R.I.P. 1961-2009

Acknowledgements

SkateLab
Becca Badillo
Gavin Badillo
Todd Huber
Scott Radinsky
Pat Ngoho
Torey Pudwill
Mike Mo Capaldi
Matt Boyster
Tom Schaar
Ben Schroeder
Curren Caples
Mark Partain
Duane Peters
Josh Nelson
Josh Borden
Anthony Janow
Cory Philips
Kristos Andrews
Brandon Read
Eric "Tuma" Britton
Ty Page
John Lucero
Eddie Hadvina
Bennet Harada
Lester Kasai
Danny Way
Mike McGill
Christian Hosoi
Lance Mountain
Steve Caballero
Tony Hawk
Skip Engblom
Lizzie Armanto
Melissa O'Grady
Bob Burnquist
Donny Barley
Dan Levy- Juice
Ivory Serra
Bob-0 Garza
Jeff Mercader
Dan Murray
Rex Heery
Benji Galloway
Lyn-Z Adams Hawkins
Dave Hackett
Ozzie Ausband
Zander Gabriel
Chris Chaput
Daniel Harold Sturt
Rob Mertz
Zach Wagner
Chris Weddle

Steve thanks these companies for their support
Santa Monica Airlines
SkateLab
DVS Shoe Company
Black Plague Wheels

Skateboard Companies
Santa Monica Airlines
Powell Peralta
Hosoi Skateboards
Dogtown
Sims
Almost
Girl
Plan B
Half Pint Skateboards
Pocket Pistols
Flip
Old Man Army
Black Label
Small Beating
Santa Cruz
G&S
Madrid
Vision
Zoo York
Birdhous

Contents

Origins

In *Legendary Tricks 2,* I write about some of the tricks that I didn't cover in the first *Legendary Tricks* book. Though the stories and photos will help give you an understanding of these legendary tricks, I still didn't cover all the tricks I wanted to write about.

You might ask, where is this trick or that trick? Everyone has his or her own opinion on what a legendary trick really is. Research and investigation into bits of skateboarding history often led to nothing more than a rumor. This meant that I had to go straight to the source or other skaters from the period for details in a lot of cases. Sometimes even the rumors faded away with the skateboarders and the tricks they made popular.

Once again I listened to legends tell their stories and share something new about skateboarding history. These are the stories and skaters that have influenced my skateboarding and me as a person. I hope this book will give you a level of appreciation for the origins of these legendary tricks and skaters that have left their mark on us all, even if you don't know it.

Steve Badillo
November 2009

Why Do I Skateboard?

I skate for peace of mind

I skate to make myself happy

I skate to make other people happy

I skate to cool down my anger

I skate to be with my friends

I skate for my parents

I skate for Santa Monica Airlines

I skate for my wife and kids

I skate to praise God

I skate to be positive in skateboarding

I skate to get my energies going

I skate to test myself ...

But I don't skate when the time isn't right

Because just then, I might take a bite.

In the mid-1980s, I got a subscription to *Thrasher Magazine* and really fell in love with skateboarding. Skateboarding at the time had a lot of colorful pro skateboarders, teams and companies. In one of those *Thrasher Magazines* was a poem written by Steve Alba, a pro for Santa Cruz Skateboards.

It struck a chord so I cut it out of the magazine and put it on my bedroom wall. It has been above my bed for some 26 years. I hope when you read this, you can relate to the words and that it will give you encouragement in your own skateboarding. Over time what I got out of this poem has changed, so I have enhanced it with a few additions.

Part 1

Early Tricks

The early skateboarding pioneers laid down the foundation of legendary tricks for younger generations to express themselves. A lot of these early tricks were based on fundamental moves. When you have a good grasp of the

fundamentals, you set yourself up to create influential skateboard tricks, and that is what these legendary skaters did.

These tricks are still being done and expanded upon by the new crop of skaters that are trying to make their mark on skateboarding. Some of the pro skaters from the 1970s are still skateboarding because it is their life. Skateboarding became the lifestyle they embraced and continue to live. Old School skateboarding *is* skateboarding, and we all appreciate what these skaters started.

01 Handstand

Handstand

Some legendary tricks have longevity — the trick was invented long ago, but you still see skateboarders doing it today. The Handstand is one of those skateboarding tricks. Even with the primitive skateboards of the early 1960s, someone, somewhere was bound to go upside down and try to ride the skateboard. What a crazy way to skateboard. Not on your feet, but in a Handstand.

It is not certain when exactly the Handstand was invented. But in 1962, Ty Page saw someone do the trick, and it inspired him to become a pro freestyler. When skateboarding starting growing in popularity in the late 1960s, a skateboard company named Makaha Skateboards invented the kicktail, giving the skateboard more leverage and ultimately creating more tricks.

The captain of the Makaha team was Bruce Logan, and he wanted Ty Page on the team, but he had to prove himself. Bruce said that Ty had to do a Handstand for four city blocks in order to make the team. So Ty found a hill in Hermosa Beach with a slight downhill angle and went for it. The Handstand, according to Ty Page, lasted at least four city blocks.

He made the team.

Ty Page's favorite place to do the Handstand was on the streets of Paris next to speeding cars with his Free Former teammate, Mark Bowden. Another skateboarder to do incredible Handstands was Steve

"Mr. Style" Tanner who did them in the streets going 35 mph (a car behind him tracked the speed). Some of the first skateboarders to do Handstands in contests were Bruce Logan and Torger Johnson during the first wave of freestyle skateboarding in the mid-1960s and early 1970s.

In the early to mid-1980s, freestyle skateboarding made a comeback. The new wave was led by gifted skateboarders like Rodney Mullen who added variations like the Fingerflip Handstand and Primo Handstand. The Fingerflip Handstand is when from a Handstand, you flip the board with your hands and land back on the board with your feet. The Primo Handstand is when from a Handstand, you flip the board with your hands and land on the rail of the skateboard. Rodney Mullen perfected these and many other freestyle tricks.

Loosen your trucks to help control the direction and correct yourself while doing a Handstand.
— *Ty Page*

The Handstand is the foundation for all the "red faced" tricks.
— *Chris Chaput*

When I played Ty Page in the movie, *Lords of Dogtown*, I had to learn the Handstand for the historic Del Mar Contest scene. I learned the trick, but it was a little sketchy. While rehearsing scenes, Stacey Peralta was watching me do the Handstand. He came up to me and showed me how the real Ty Page would do it. I took Stacey's advice, and the trick became easier to do and looked a lot better. Thanks, Stacey.

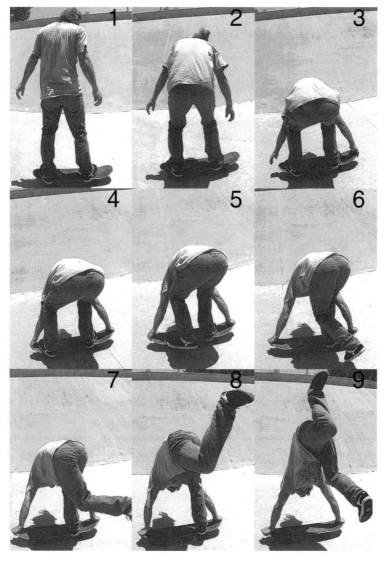

You should be able to do a Handstand before trying it on a skateboard. Start off by pushing with medium to fast speed. Reach down and grab both the nose and tail of the skateboard. While moving, kick your back foot up and over your head.

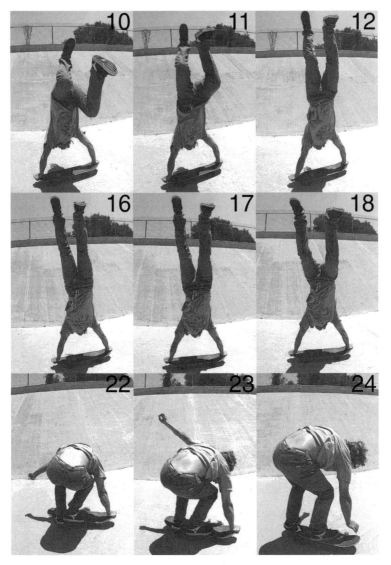

Bring your other foot up and match your feet together up over your head. Use your hands to control the direction of the skateboard, tilting left or right. Hold the Handstand as long as you can.

When ready to land, start to bring your feet down to the board one at a time. Spread your feet out and stand up. Sweet. Now try it with a Fingerflip!

Chris Chaput, V-sit Handstand

01. Handstand photo credits
Still photo: Ty Page
Still photo: Ty Page and Mark Bowden
Still photo: Steve Badillo playing Ty Page
Still photo: Chris Chaput, V-sit Handstand / Photographer: Bill Deeble
Sequence: Steve Badillo, Handstand / Photographer: Gavin Badillo

02 Daffy
Yeah Right Manual

Daffy (Yeah Right Manual)
In the late 1960s and early 1970s, freestyle was driving skateboarding, and the man that was in the driver's seat was Ty "Mr. Incredible" Page. During Ty's career, he invented many tricks and won a lot of skateboard contests with his fast footwork and technique. His style was such a blur that in order to photograph him, skateboard magazines were forced to buy faster cameras to keep up with his pace. His skateboard routines were amazing combinations of many different elements.

In 1974 Ty added a new trick to his routine, the Daffy. While skateboarding with some high-school friends, Ty was doing Nose Wheelies, One-Footed Tail Wheelies and 360 Wheelies. He then got the idea to put two boards together and try Wheelies. It worked — one foot on the nose of one board and the other foot on the tail of the other board and skate in a Wheelie (as it was known back then). One day while Ty was doing this two-foot, two-board Wheelie, another well-respected freestyle pro skater named

> *Even though I invented it, I like the name Yeah Right Manual better than the Daffy.*
> *— Ty Page*

Russ Howell saw this and called the trick a "Daffy" because it resembled a skier doing a Daffy in the air. Soon many pro freestylers added the Daffy to their routines, and it became a crowd pleaser. Ty's favorite place to do the Daffy was in Paris while on tour in Europe.

More than 20 years after Ty had invented the Daffy, it had a renewed popularity with the influential Girl skate video, *Yeah Right*. The legendary street skater, Eric Koston, did the Daffy in the skate flick and kids all over America said, "Look at that Yeah Right Manual Eric did." In the mid 1980s Wheelies were no longer known as Wheelies, but instead were called Manuals. Then a whole new generation of skaters renamed it the Yeah Right Manual. Activision's *Tony Hawk Underground* video game added it as a special trick and called it the Yeah Right Manual, as well.

In 2005 Hollywood brought skateboarding to life in the film, *Lords of Dogtown,* where I played the role of Ty Page. In some of my scenes, I do the Daffy at the re-creation of the Del Mar Skate Contest, where in real life Ty Page placed second. It was a privilege for me to learn some of the old freestyle tricks including the Daffy, Handstand, Headstand and others.

Daffy

The Daffy is a Manual trick, so have lots of flat ground while learning. You will need two boards to make it work. Place one board out in front of you and the other board ready to roll. Push with lots of speed (the faster you go the farther you will Manual) placing

02. Daffy (Yeah Right Manual) photo credits
Sequence: Steve Badillo, Daffy / Photographer: Gavin Badillo

20

your front foot on the back tail of board number one. As you approach the second board, place your back foot on the nose of board number two. Then at the same time, both boards should go into Manuals, one Nose Manual and one Tail Manual.

Stretch your arms out for balance and hold it as long as possible. When you lose speed and want to end the trick, let go of the board with your back foot (which is in the Nose Manual) and place it on the nose of the original board in front. Then swing the board 180 to come out straight and roll away.

03 Acid Drop / Bomb Drop

Lyn-Z Adams Hawkins,
Acid Drop

Acid Drop / Bomb Drop
The Acid Drop and the Bomb Drop are very similar to each other. That is why I present them together for the stories and photos. These two tricks have inspired old and new skateboarders for years.

Duane Peters invented the Acid Drop around 1975 or 1976 in an empty pool by rolling into it perpendicular to the coping. When you do an Acid Drop, you air into the pool and land near the bottom of the transition, which makes this trick scary. This trick encouraged other skaters to roll in ramps and pools frontside and backside and Manual into and out of bowls. Duane, to this day, performs Acid Drops in contest and demos.

It's a little vague on who was the first to do the Bomb Drop. Any skater in the 1960s who picked up a board and jumped on it could have been the first — and many skaters did just that.

What makes this trick legendary is that although skateboarders started Bomb Dropping off curbs, they eventually took on higher and higher obstacles. In the 1970s it was off broken refrigerators and ledges. In the 1980s it was off rooftops and cars.

Then in the 1990s, Danny Way really stepped it up by Bomb Dropping out of a helicopter onto a vert ramp. That was the highest recorded Bomb Drop until Danny decided to put the record out of reach for everybody and perhaps for all time.

The actual measurements of his drop include a 28-foot free fall into a 56-foot ramp for a total of 82 feet 3 inches.

Insane. Danny Way is legend.

He set a new world record at the Hard Rock Café in Las Vegas in 2006 by Bomb Dropping off the building's guitar into a vertical quarter pipe. The actual measurements of his drop include a 28-foot free fall into a 56-foot ramp for a total of 82 feet 3 inches.

Insane. Danny Way is legend.

Danny Way Bomb Dropping to a world record in 2006 at the Hard Rock Café, Las Vegas, Nevada.

Instructions for Acid Drop

The Acid Drop is usually done in a pool, bowl or ramp. You stand on your board on the top of the deck of the bowl and roll into it by lifting the nose slightly as you roll over the coping straight on. Do not roll in frontside or backside at slight angles.

This trick is done straight in. As you lift the nose, lean into the transition with your head.

You should air into the transition before hitting the bottom tranny and flatbottom. Stand up and straighten your legs.

03. Acid Drop and Bomb Drop photo credits
Still photo: Lyn-Z Adams Hawkins, Acid Drop / Photographer: Steve Badillo
Still photo: Danny Way, Bomb Drop, Hard Rock Café / Photographer: Getty Images
Sequence: Cory Philips, Bomb Drop / Photographer: Steve Badillo

The Bomb Drop can be done almost anywhere there is a gap or up high onto a bank, flat ground or ramp. Grab either the nose, backside or Indy grab before you begin. Plant your back foot and leap out with your front foot ready to be placed on the front bolts.

While falling, lean forward and place your back foot onto the back bolts. As you land, compress with your knees to absorb the shock and continue to lean forward.

Start with something small like a curb or small ledge and work your way up to the top of the Hard Rock Café guitar.

04 Slappy

Slappy

Who was the first to do a Slappy? Where was it done? That is like asking who the first skateboarder was. In the early to mid-1970s, surfers were skateboarders and tried to surf the concrete. Using surf style slashes and turns, skate-boarders started hitting tops of banks, curbs or any type of lip trying to grind the wave. Before the Ollie, skaters would bash into curbs and try to get wheel bite to slash grind the lip. This led to skaters going up curbs through grinds.

One of the earliest pro skaters to popularize the Slappy was John Lucero in 1979. He started doing Slappies on the curbs in front of his house. First doing it backside and then frontside, John had a lot of style while doing the trick and later added variations to it.

I think Corey O'Brien and some of his friends from NorCal were also doing them around the same time.
— John Lucero

Slappies were part of the beginning of street skating, as a common go-to trick that inspired many more grinds and slides. The best curbs to do a Slappy? The ones painted red.

You can do a Slappy either frontside or backside and is usually done on curbs or parking blocks. Ride up to the curb with medium speed at a slight angle. If you are doing it frontside, lean on your heelside of the board.

You almost want to wheel bite to slap the trucks onto the curb. Start with your front truck, then back truck, get on sideways with the board and tilt the board on top of the curb.

Lean forward and grind a 50/50. When you are ready to come off, lift the nose up and pull the board away from the curb.

Anything that had a lip became a wave to us ... something to do to go up curbs.
— Mark Partain

04. Slappy photo credits
Sequence: Steve Badillo, Frontside Slappy / Photographer: Gavin Badillo

05 Manual Roll

Pat Ngoho, Manual Roll

Manual Roll

Before the trick was called the Manual Roll, it was called a Wheelie — skidding your tail while the nose was up. Skaters from the 1960s used the Wheelie as a staple trick. Then freestyle skaters did Nose Wheelies, Tail Wheelies, One-Foot Wheelies and other tricks. But it wasn't until the combination of airing out of a bowl into a Manual and then Acid Dropping back into the bowl that the trick Manual Roll was invented. Then the silly Wheelie became a scary bowl trick.

In 1979 a young Pat Ngoho was skateboarding at Marina Skatepark and was progressing his skateboarding. Taking tricks that he saw other pro skateboarders perform, he created his own tricks. Crazy grom skaters were trying to imitate the pros they saw at the skateparks who were inventing tricks every day. Ngoho would roll out of the bowls, up on to the deck and then roll back into them.

I never really laid claim to the trick until Cab called it out, "That's your trick, you were the first to do it."
— Pat Ngoho

Then one day he added the Wheelie to it by rolling out of the bowl into a Wheelie and then rolling back into the bowl.

The Manual Roll was created. But Ngoho did not think much of it until Steve Caballero said to Pat that he was the first to fly out of a bowl Manual and roll back in. Many variations have spawned from the Manual, especially street skating tricks and BMX riding.

05. Manual Roll photo credits
Sequence: Pat Ngoho, Manual Roll / Photographer: Steve Badillo

You need to know how to roll out of and roll into ramps or bowls. Also, you must be proficient with Manuals. Skate up the transition with enough speed to launch out of the bowl and onto the deck. Make sure you launch out at an angle, either frontside or

backside, to help start the Manual. When you hit the coping, use it to help air into the Manual. Keep your feet spread. Then as you start your Manual, use your arms to help your balance. Lean on the back truck.

As you start to slow down, ride back to the coping and roll in at an angle. Lean forward toward the transition and stand up. Then try it Nose Manual.

Chapter 05

Part 2

Duane Peters

The "Master of Disaster" Duane Peters is a skateboard icon. He has helped influence and shape skateboarding through his creative and aggressive style of skating. He invented the Sweeper, Acid Drop, Disaster, Indy Air, Layback Roll Out, Fakie Thruster, Backside Layback Grind Revert, Invert Revert and Loop of Death. Peters helped popularize along with others the Layback Grind, Footplants and Fastplants.

Skateboarding and punk rock go hand in hand and Duane Peters epitomizes them both. This legendary skater has not only influenced skateboarding, but also the punk rock scene with his numerous bands. As one of the first skaters to embrace punk rock and skateboarding as a lifestyle, his fashion with clothes, hair cut and attitude started trends that are now mainstream. Duane is still skateboarding and playing music, entering contests and demos, and even has a biographic film from the skateboard company that sponsors him, Black Label Skateboards. It's titled *Who Cares: The Duane Peters Story.*

06 Sweeper

Sweeper

The late 1970s was a golden era for pool skating. Many new tricks were being created and at the forefront was the legendary skater, Duane Peters. Duane invented one of my favorite lip tricks — the Sweeper.

The Sweeper gets its name from the motion of grabbing the nose of the board and sweeping it along the deck, clearing out anyone standing near the coping. Duane first did the trick around 1978 in an empty pool. Like most of his tricks, he uses unusual grabs on the lip of the ramp. One variation is to grab with your crail hand, therefore altering the name from Sweeper to Creeper. Rob Roskopp made the cover of *Thrasher Magazine* in November 1983 doing the Sweeper at the Midwest Melee contest.

The first time I did a Sweeper was on my friend's vert ramp, which we youthfully called the "Ramp of the Gods." My friend Daniel Sabelis showed me how to do the trick in 1988. At first, I could do the sweeping motion to tail, but had a hard time committing to the drop. Daniel said think of it as dropping in by grabbing the nose. I finally landed it with his advice.

Duane Peters

The Sweeper gets its name from the motion of grabbing the nose of the board and sweeping it along the deck, clearing out anyone standing near the coping.

06. Sweeper photo credits
Still photo: Duane Peters headshot / Photographer: Steve Badillo
Sequence: Steve Badillo, Sweeper / Photographer: Gavin Badillo

Sweepers are done in ramps, bowls, ditches or pools. Skate with plenty of speed to get to the top of the deck of the ramp. Float frontside as you grab the nose of the board with your forward hand. Next, plant your back foot on the coping of the ramp.

Keep your front foot on the board as you swing the
board frontside. Lay the tail down on the coping as
you hop back into transition landing on the tail. Lean
and compress down the ramp.

07 Disaster

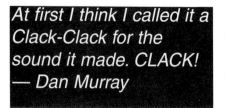

At first I think I called it a Clack-Clack for the sound it made. CLACK! — Dan Murray

Disaster

Some tricks evolve over time but don't achieve their full potential and become legendary until other skaters take the trick and add their own 180 twist. That may be the case regarding Duane Peters and Dan Murray with the Disaster.

A Florida skater named Dan Murray may have been the first to do the Fakie Hang Up in 1978 at Cadillac Wheels Skateboard Concourse in Lighthouse Point, Florida. The Fakie Hang Up is what led to the Disaster, as told by Dan. Dan and Chuck Lagana started doing them in the shallow end of the Monster Hole pool by fakieing up, rocking over, grabbing the tail and pulling it back in. The no-handed version named by Shogo Kobo as The Fakie Hang Up (at Cherry Hill in 1979) came later. They morphed it from Fakie Hang Up into the Disaster during the summer of 1978.

When Alan Gelfand and Dan came to California for the first time, Stacy Peralta asked Alan to show him the Ollie. Until then, California skaters had not seen one. Stacy was courting him for Powell, and since Dan was only 18, he was kind of Alan's chaperone.

They were at Paramount Skatepark, at the end of the halfpipe, when Dan took an L-corner and ended in a round bowl. Stacy saw Dan do the Hand Grabbing Fakie Hang Up and how he was slapping the board. He said, "Hey, I bet you could make it. Why don't you

Dan Murray, Fakie Hang Up

try doing that no handed?" So Dan rolled up, slapped extra hard, the board bounced back, he took the weight off his back foot, the wheels cleared the lip with only a slight hang and Dan rode it out. He made it! By the end of the California trip, Dan was doing the trick consistently.

Later that same year (1978), the "Master of Disaster" Duane Peters added a 180 to the trick, making it the Disaster skaters are familiar with today. Duane continues to do them in contests and demos. Duane also did the Fakie Disaster version of the trick — meaning not just a Fakie Hang Up, but bouncing off the coping and getting a little air then smacking the middle of the board and coming in forward.

The Disaster is one of those lip tricks that is not very flashy, but is done by most skaters on almost every type of terrain there is. It's a versatile trick used by transition and street skaters alike. It is combined with other maneuvers to create variations like the Variel Disaster, Nosepick Disaster, Blunt Disaster, Kickflip Disaster, Air to Disaster and about a thousand other combinations.

The Disaster is done either frontside or backside. It is usually done on the lip of a ramp, pool or ditch. Ride up the transition with enough speed to hit the lip of the ramp. As you hit the lip, either float or Ollie Backside 180. Try to bounce the back wheels off the

coping to help rotate the board 180. Land the board on the coping in the middle of the skateboard. Your feet should be spread on the board. Start leaning toward the transition. Put some weight on the nose to lift the tail and clear the coping. You don't want to

hang up on the coping while coming back into the ramp. Stand up and roll away, then try it frontside.

07. Disaster photo credits
Still Photo: Dan Murray, Fakie Hang Up
Sequence: Steve Badillo, Disaster / Photographer: Gavin Badillo

08 Layback Grind

Layback Grind

Surfing heavily influenced most early skateboard tricks. Surfing style gives skateboarding its flow and slashes. This is particularly true with the Layback Grind. It has a long evolution — from skateboarders first doing Bertslides on banks and ditches, imitating surf slashes on waves and then taking it to the deep

end of pools Bertsliding up to the tile.

Some of the first skaters to put their hands way below the coping and slash out at the lip were Jay Smith (who was an original Bones Brigade member), John Stevenson and "Rubberman" Larry Bertleman in the mid-to-late 1970s. The next step was to take it to the coping with the hand and the grind in the Layback position. Duane Peters first did this in 1979.

Many different variations came from the Layback Grind like Duane Peters's Layback Roll Out where his hand is on the coping and the board is on the deck as he pulls it back in. Later in 1979, Eddie "El Gato" Elguera did the backside version of the Layback. Some skaters also did Layback Grind to Tail and dropped back in.

Other pros later stepped it up, like Allen Losi who would do Layback Smith Grinds. Skaters like Kevin "The Worm" Anderson and Kevin Reed combined the Ollie with it, by Ollieing into the Layback Grind — sick! In the 1980s, other pro skaters who helped popularize the trick with their style in contests and demos were Christian Hosoi, Dave Hackett and Mike Smith.

Surfing style gives skateboarding its flow and slashes. This is particularly true with the Layback Grind.

08. Layback Grind photo credits
Sequence: Duane Peters, Layback Grind / Photographer: Steve Badillo
Sequence: Mark Partain, Layback Grind / Photographer: Steve Badillo

Duane Peters, Layback Grind

Mark Partain, Layback Grind

You should learn Frontside Grinds and Frontside Bertslides before trying Layback Grinds. Layback Grinds are usually done in ramps and bowls. Skate up to the coping with plenty of speed and at an angle to help start the Frontside Grind. As you start your

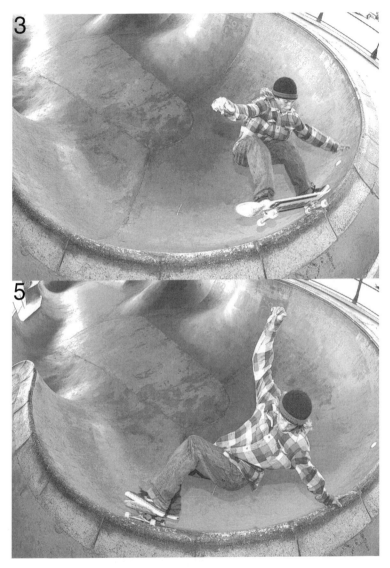

Frontside Grind, lean back and reach down with your back hand to grab the coping. Extend your grind, leaning on your hand. To land the trick, ride down the transition and push off the coping with your hand. Stand up and try it backside.

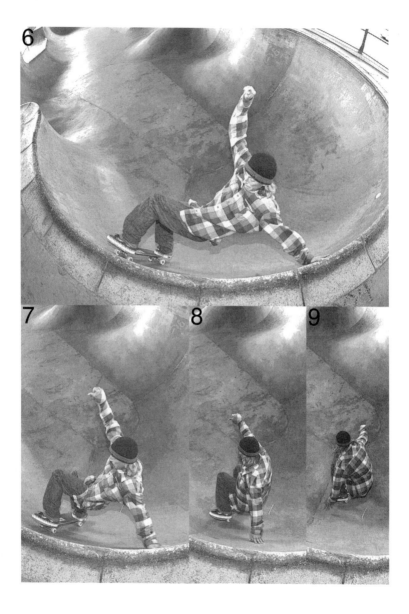

09 The Loop

Dave Hackett

The Loop

The Loop has got to be one of the most insane legendary tricks that skateboarders have done. Only a handful of skateboarders have landed the Loop, but many more dream of doing it.

The first skater to do the Loop was Duane Peters in 1978. He was 16 years old and did it for a big Hollywood production show. They wanted him to do the trick while a multimillion dollar laser show was going on. The ramp was on the way to the studio when it fell off the truck on a freeway and became warped like an egg. While rehearsing, Duane landed it a few times, but then he fell and broke his collarbone. He kept going for a second Loop and flew off, breaking his collarbone again. The next day Duane went back to the ramp with a collar-bone brace and started doing Fakies on it. But the producers freaked out and banned him from skating any more for fear of being sued. Duane called that particular Loop the "Loop of Death."

In 1996, almost 20 later, Tony Hawk built a highly speciazied Loop ramp and landed the first Loop since Duane Peters. The first ramp Tony built was really sketchy. It was made of wood with imperfect dimensions. It's amazing that Tony landed the Loop at all. Then Tony made an improved Loop ramp that

he used for his Boom Boom Huck Jam skateboarding show. This ramp made it possible for a handful of other skaters to land the trick.

Slowly more and more pro skaters wanted to try the Loop. In 2003, filming for the Firm's skate video, Bob Burnquist was the first skater to do the Loop from the fakie position. He broke his foot while filming the trick. Later that same year, Bob became the first to do a full Loop with a top section of the fullpipe missing. So he did a Loop and aired the top of the fullpipe — insane! He topped that by becoming the only skater to do the Loop switch stance.

In 2006, Dave Hackett became the oldest pro skate-boarder to do Tony Hawk's Loop at the age of 46 — a feat that is legendary in itself. Before Dave did the Loop, he was inspired by Daniel Sturt, who at the time was the oldest skater to do the Loop at 38. Daniel pulled Dave aside and coached him on the stance, speed and positioning of doing the trick. Dave recalls that if it weren't for Daniel Sturt, he would not have pulled off the Loop of Death.

The Loop Club includes many skaters and continues to grow. The club now has 17 members including Duane Peters, Tony Hawk, Bam, Al Partanen, Peter Hewitt, Lincoln Ueda, Sergie Ventura, Bob Burnquist, Jake Brown, Andy MacDonald, Bucky Lasek, Daniel Sturt, Jeff Grosso, Jason Ellis, Alex Chalmers, Josh Borden and Dave Hackett.

The Loop of Death is not a trick. It is one of the heaviest stunts in skateboarding because it defies a number of Universal Laws — specifically, the Law of Gravity.
— Dave Hackett

09. Loop photo credits
Still Photo: Steve Badillo, Fakie / Photographer: Jeff Mercader
Still Photo: Dave Hackett, Loop / Photographer: Daniel Harold Sturt

Instructions

Do not try to do the Loop unless you are good
enough, know your limits and are friends with Tony
Hawk.

Part 3

Inverts

Of all the skateboard tricks done by millions of skaters around the world, Inverts stand out among them all. All skaters can do tricks — Airs, Grinds, Slides, Lip Tricks and Carves — but when you put your hand on the coping and do an Invert, it separates you from the others.

Bobby Valdez was the first skater to learn the mechanics of Inverts, and since then, many variations have been created. These are some of the legendary Inverts and skaters that I think must be

included in the pantheon of skateboarding.

10 Eggplant

Lance Mountain

Eggplant

The artistic duo of Lance Mountain and Neil Blender have left their impression on skateboarding in terms of progression, style and personal expression. In a little bowl in 1980, Lance and Neil were playing the skate game Add On, where one skater does a trick and the next skater has to do that trick and add another trick.They were doing Invert variations, when Lance did an Invert, but with the opposite hands grabbing the coping and board.

Neil was next to do the trick when he called out "Egg Plant" in his great sarcastic voice. The trick was just that — stinky like a rotten egg. Then they took the Eggplant to a vert ramp and got it wired. Lance found that if he threw it up like an Indy Air and committed to go upside down, he could rotate over and land near his plant hand to make a smoother landing. After that, the Eggplant name stuck.

Around that time, Gator was doing something he called the "Roto-rooter." This is an Eggplant where you plant a hand and rotate on the inside of it Ally-oop style. In October 1984, Neil Blender made the cover of *Thrasher Magazine* doing the Eggplant.

Sickest Eggplant I ever saw was Gonz on the extension for about four seconds in 1991 at the Transitions Skatepark.
— Ben Schroeder

This trick is legendary because it allows skaters to stylize the move. A skater can physically accent the trick with his or her own personality. The Eggplant can be fully stalled and tweaked, not to mention that you use the opposite hand on the coping. This Invert is one of the most difficult to execute.

Other pros that made the Eggplant look good were Mike McGill, Mike Crescini, Jeff Grosso, Ben Schroeder and Remy Stratton.

10. Eggplant photo credits
Sequence: Lance Mountain, Eggplant
Photographer: Steve Badillo

The Eggplant is an Invert, but with a twist. You switch
hands on where you would grab the board and the
coping. This Invert is usually done on ramps and in
pools. Ride straight up the transition with medium
speed leaning a little toward backside. Keep your

feet spread. As you hit the lip, grab the board with your Indy hand in the tuck knee position. With your forward hand, grab the coping. Look down the transition as the board comes up and you start to stall on your forward hand. Stall the Eggplant around until

the nose of the board can come back down on or near where your hand stalled the Invert. Let go of the coping and air back into the transition. Stand up.

11
Frontside Invert

Eric "Tuma" Britton, Frontside Invert

Frontside Invert

The Frontside Invert is a very stylish Invert that goes back to the late 1970s and very early 1980s. I asked Eddie "El Gato" Elguera who was the first to do it and Eddie said he saw Steve Schneer do a Frontside Invert around 1978. But Steve never did them much after that.

Soon after Eddie saw Steve Schneer do the trick, El Gato set out to learn it for himself. Dale "Sausage Man" Smith coached Eddie and helped show him the mechanics. In 1980, Eddie Elguera became Skater of the Year for the second time, winning the Gold Cup Series and World Championships with the mastered Frontside Invert as one of his go-to tricks. That year, Elguera popularized the trick and many skateboarders followed his lead.

One skater who used the Frontside Invert to showcase his abilities was a young Steve Caballero. He did them in contests and at skateparks like Upland Skatepark. Magazines featured shots of Steve doing this trick and everyone tried to copy his style.

He did them all the way over with the tips of his toes on the board over his head, looking like he would almost fall into the transition. This was later considered the classic style of a Frontside Invert.

Frontside Invert became one of the most coveted Inverts because fewer people were able to do them right.
— Lance Mountain

11. Frontside Invert photo credits
Still Photo: Eddie "El Gato" Elguera, headshot / Photographer: Steve Badillo
Still Photo: Steve Caballero, Frontside Invert / Photographer: Steve Badillo
Sequence: Eric "Tuma" Britton, Frontside Invert / Photographer: Steve Badillo

Frontside Invert

Eddie "El Gato" Elguera

Steve Caballero, Frontside Invert

You should learn Frontside Airs before trying Frontside Inverts. Roll up the transition with medium speed at a slight frontside angle. As you smack the lip, grab the board with your Indy hand, and with your forward hand, reach down and grab the coping.

Throw the board up and over above your head. Put your weight on your Invert hand. Stall the Invert and re-enter the transition near the spot where your hand grabbed the coping. Air back down under the coping and stand up.

12 Phillips 66

Josh Borden, Phillips 66

Phillips 66

A giant in the vertical skateboarding world throughout the 1980s was Jeff Phillips. The tall, aggressive, progressive and powerful pro skater from Texas influenced the skateboard community with his burly Boneless and his intimidating painted skull helmet.

As the vert contest wars were being fought between Tony Hawk and Christian Hosoi, Jeff Phillips was destroying ramps in Texas where he had his own skatepark. Quietly doing his own thing, Jeff was doing tricks with variations — especially with Inverts, Texas Plants and his Stiff Leg Airs. He also got the cover of *Thrasher* in January 1985 doing a monster Frontside Boneless. Jeff always did his tricks bigger and faster than everyone else. I think that is why he left such an impression on other skateboarders.

Not many vert pros do it because of the high degree of difficulty, but that's why it's a legendary trick. When you see a Phillips 66, you get blown away!

One day Jeff was skating with a younger Shawn Peddie from Walker Skateboards. Shawn busted out a Fakie 360 Invert on the vert ramp and Jeff learned

Jeff Phillips, Phillips 66

the trick that day. Jeff, being one of those pro skaters in the top 10 at every vert contest he entered, took this Fakie 360 Invert and made it his own. Calling the trick the Phillips 66 after gas stations in Texas, Jeff popularized it by using it in his contest runs. Whenever Jeff was asked about the Phillips 66, he would credit Shawn Peddie as the guy who actually invented it.

In Texas everything is big and the Phillips 66 trick is hard to pull off. Not many vert pros do it because of the high degree of difficulty, but that's why it's a legendary trick. When you see a Phillips 66, you get blown away!

The Phillips 66 is a combination of a Caballerial and an Invert. They are usually done in pools or ramps. You start off skating fakie with enough speed to do a Caballerial toward the lip of the ramp. As you skate fakie, bounce your wheels off the coping to help start

the fakie 360 rotation. Turn your head and shoulders to help rotate. When you blast off the coping, reach down and grab the board in the mute position with your forward hand. Then with your back hand, reach for the coping to do the Invert part of the trick. Rotate

the nose all the way around 360 back to the transition. Land under the coping skating forward and stand up. Now try it with your eyes closed.

Part 4

Vert Airs

The audience at vert contests or demos cheer, "Catch some Air!" They say this because when you experience a vert contest, the biggest Airs get the biggest cheers. How exciting those Airs are!

Most of these tricks were invented in the 1980s when vert skating became the showcase of the skateboard world with skaters such as Tony Hawk, Steve Caballero, Mike McGill, Lance Mountain, Chris Miller, Micke Alba, Lester Kasai, Christian Hosoi and others. Vert skating of the '80s was the foundation of the Super Park, Mega-Ramp and vert contests of today. With the degree of difficulty at the insane level, today's vert skaters are pushing a standard that is mind bending.

13 Mute Air

Tom Schaar, Mute Air

I was told that Alan Losi's father, Gil Losi, named my trick Mute Air (that I pulled out frontside at the Pro/Am event at Ranch in 1981) because I am always quiet and talk funny because I am hard of hearing.
— Chris Weddle

Mute Air

Things that attract people to skateboarding are its varied styles and the many ways for people to express themselves. You can take a normal Backside Air, try a different grab and it becomes a new trick. Put a little style into it and you feel good. That is what happened with this legendary trick.

In the case of the Mute Air, a young skater from the 1980s named Chris Weddle was learning Backside Airs. Instead of the normal backside grab, he used the same hand, but grabbed the other side of the board. In 1981, just a week before a pro contest, he invented the Mute Air as a new trick to add to his run. He perfected it at Ranch Skatepark in Colton, California. Alan Losi's father, Gil Losi, noticed Chris doing the Air and walked into the skate shop and started talking about it. Chris's dad overheard Gil and said, "That's my boy, the mute kid. You know, the deaf guy." By the end of the conversation the new trick was called the Mute Air. Because of his hearing disability, Chris was not always the most talkative guy in the park. The trick has spawned many variations and is now one of the most common grabs in skateboarding.

13. Mute Air photo credits
Sequence: Tom Schaar, Mute Air / Photographer: Steve Badillo

Before trying Mute Airs, you should first learn Backside Airs. Mute Airs are done on ramps and in pools. Skate up the transition with medium to fast speed. Ride straight up the ramp and smack the coping with the back wheels to help blast the Air.

Chapter 13

Grab Mute with your forward hand on the toe side of the board, behind your front foot. Start rotating backside 180 as you turn the nose around. Look for the transition and a spot to land just under the coping. Compress and stand up.

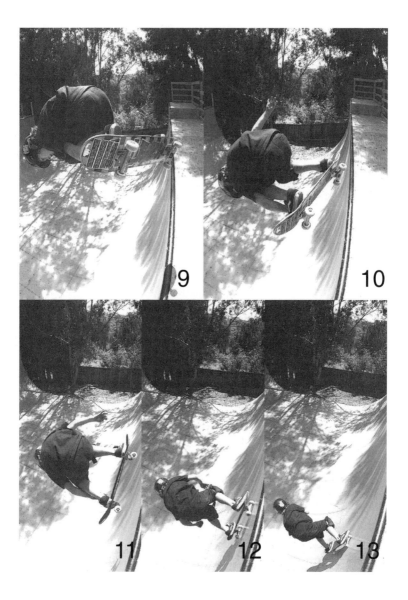

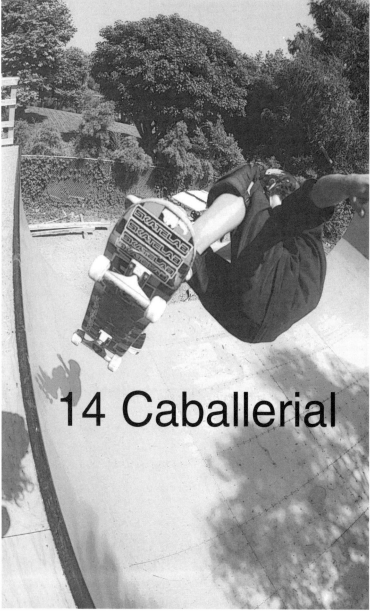

14 Caballerial

Tom Schaar, Caballerial

Caballerial

When you talk about legendary skaters, one of the first names that comes to mind is Steve Caballero. A true ambassador for skateboarding and accomplished musician, Steve has seen it all through the professional skateboarder's eyes.

Steve was sponsored by Powell Peralta in 1978, and at the age of 15, became a loyal member of the legendary Bones Brigade. Caballero's entrance into the pro arena was in 1980 at the Gold Cup series at the Oasis Skatepark. Later that same year, Steve Caballero invented the Caballerial, which is a Fakie 360 Air or Ollie. It is also known as the Full Cab.

Steve got the idea for this trick from professional skater and friend, Robert "The Fly" Schlaefli. Cab learned it in the bowl at Winchester Skatepark in Campbell, California, where he was a local skateboarder.

One day he was watching The Fly do a Fakie 360 Kickturn in the keyhole pool, but he was going really fast and flew out of the bowl as he bailed. Caballero thought to himself, "Maybe this could be possible to do if I just bonked my back wheels off the coping doing a Fakie Ollie and holding my legs in long enough to get all the way around. Then I might be able to land it."

After visualizing the trick and practicing it in the bowl for a month, he landed it, making skateboard history. Later, he showed the trick to Stacy Peralta and other Bones Brigade members in a contest at Marina Del Rey Skatepark. Stacey called it the Caballerial.

Caballero also was the first skater to have his own skate shoe. Steve's signature Vans shoe is also called the Half Cab. The Half Cab was manufactured by Vans Shoes and has remained their highest selling and longest running model.

Caballero thought to himself, "Maybe this could be possible to do if I just bonked my back wheels off the coping doing a Fakie Ollie and holding my legs in long enough to get all the way around. Then I might be able to land it."

Though the Caballerial was first done in a pool, it can be done in both street and vert skating or backside and frontside. Half of the Caballerial is called Half Cab, which is a Fakie 180 Air or Ollie.

14. Caballerial photo credits
Still Photo: Steve Caballero
Still Photo: Steve Caballero Caballerial / Photographer: Steve Badillo
Sequence: Tom Schaar, Caballerial / Photographer: Steve Badillo

Tony Hawk checks out Steve Caballero doing his signature trick.

The Caballerial is a Fakie 360 Air or Ollie. You will approach the lip of the ramp fakie with medium to fast speed. Have your feet in the Ollie position and as you reach the lip, snap your Ollie and bounce the wheels off the coping rotating your head and shoul-

ders backside. Keep rotating the nose until you come around 360 leaning toward the bottom transition. Compress and stand up. You may want to try this trick on flat ground before you try it on a ramp. This trick can be done both backside and frontside.

15 Judo Air

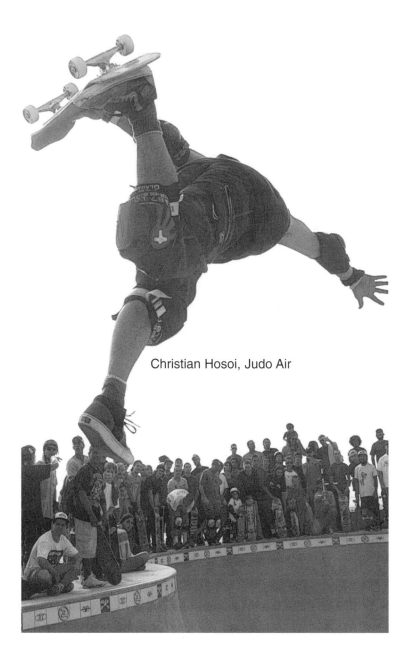

Christian Hosoi, Judo Air

Lester Kasai, Judo Air

15. Judo Air photo credits
Still photo: Christian Hosoi, Judo Air / Photographer Gavin Badillo
Still photo: Lester Kasai, Judo Air / Photographer: Steve Badillo
Still photo: Steve Caballero and Tony Hawk / Photographer: Steve Badillo
Sequence: Steve Badillo, Judo Air / Photographer: Gavin Badillo

Judo Air

The Judo Air is a tricked out skateboard maneuver where you kick your front foot forward during a Backside Air. The first pro skateboarder to do this trick was Micke Alba, the younger brother of Steve Alba, around 1982 or 1983. Soon after seeing Micke do the trick, other pro skaters — like Tony Hawk, Christian Hosoi, Steve Caballero and Lester Kasai — also popularized it. Tony Hawk took the Judo Air even further by kicking out the tail foot, a trick later called the Airwalk.

Though at first the Judo Air was called a One-Footed Air, it was evenutally labeled the Judo Air because the skater performed the so-called karate kick. Lester Kasai might have been the skater to call it the Judo.

The Judo Air made the cover of *Thrasher Magazine* with Jesse Martinez launching off a ramp in July 1986. Because of numerous ads and articles, the Judo Air became a popular trick for both vert and street skating and continues to be used by today's pro skaters in contests and demos.

Cab and Hosoi, they were the ones. They would hold their heads. Looks good in a photo.
— Lance Mountain

The trick has stayed in the repertoire of many top skaters including Lance Mountain, who did it in an Independent ad shot at the 2009 opening of the new addition to Lincoln City Skatepark.

Steve Caballero and Tony Hawk

You should learn Backside Airs before trying Judo
Airs. Judos can be done in ramps, over hips, on
launch ramps, down stairs, over gaps and transfers.
Approach the lip with lots of speed, as if you were
doing a Backside Air. Grab the board backside either

behind or above your front foot near the nose. Blast your air and grab the board, then kick out your front foot into the Judo position. To get the full Judo, kick your foot out quickly, extend it and then bring it back to the board.

Think karate kick and just do it. When you bring the front foot back, land on the bolts and ride down the transition.

16 Stalefish

Stalefish

Tony Hawk has been arguably the most important skater in skateboard history. Inventing nearly 90 skateboarding tricks, his influence is pervasive throughout the world of skating and the world at large. With all the success Tony has had, it is hard to narrow down what trick is legendary. Of course the 900, Madonna, Airwalk and other tricks Tony has invented are legendary (read *Skateboarding: Legendary Tricks*), but the Stalefish stands out as an unusual grab for an Air.

When you see a skater do a Stalefish it gets your attention. Tony first conceived this grab after all the other grab Airs had been invented. He dedicated serious time to its visualization and finally landed it in 1985 at a summer camp in Stockholm, Sweden.

During that tour, Tony kept a daily journal of events, what he was eating and so forth. A camper asked if Stalefish was the strange grab Tony had been trying (in reality, stale fish was the description of a meal served at camp).

Tony Hawk had been working on the new grab, but it did not have a name yet. So Tony named the new grab Stalefish. Despite the stale fish for lunch that no one was eating, there was lots of great skate-boarding.

Stale fish was the description of a meal served at camp.

16. Stalefish photo credits
Still photo: Tony Hawk surprise / Photographer: Steve Badillo
Still photo: Steve Badillo, Stalefish / Photographer: Gavin Badillo
Sequence: Curren Caples, Stalefish / Photographer: Steve Badillo

Chapter 16

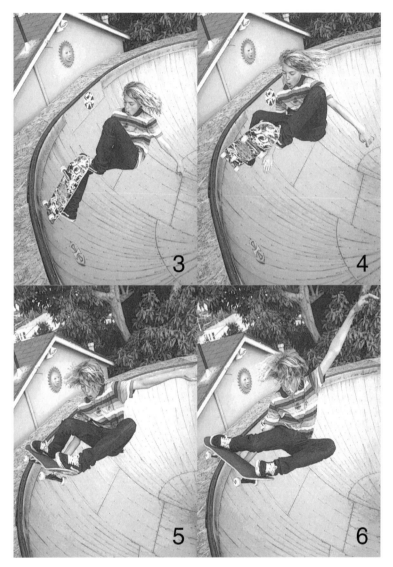

The Stalefish can be done on ramps, bowls and hips. Skate as fast as you would for a Frontside Air, but instead of grabbing the board Indy, grab the board with your Indy hand behind your back between your heels. You will need to Ollie off the coping to get a

little bit higher to do the Stalefish. Reach down, grab Stalefish and bend your knees to help the grab and air back to the transition. Spot your landing in the transition and compress.

17 McTwist

Matt Boyster, McTwist

McTwist

One of the most legendary tricks of all time is the McTwist. The McTwist has lasted the test of time and is widely used by most vert professional skateboarders.

While on a skateboard tour in Europe, Mike McGill, along with others from the legendary Bones Brigade team, stopped in Sweden at a skatecamp. Mike was skating with the kids at the camp when he saw a roller skater named Fred Blood grab his skates and do 540 rotations on the vert ramp. This inspired Mike to attempt 540 Airs. Mike first started doing flat 540 spins grabbing Mute, then later added the inverted "McTwist" part of the trick. This means, as Mike was rotating 540, he would invert his body with the board over his head instead of a flat spin. This gave the trick a unique twist and made it a favorite for both skaters and audience. After Mike landed it, the next skater to do it was Lester Kasai, then Tony Hawk, Lance Mountain and others. When Rodney Mullen saw the trick, he named it the McTwist using Mike's last name and the twisting motion that the move uoco.

Since that day in the summer of 1984, the McTwist has opened up a dimension in vertical skateboarding

Mike McGill, McTwist

> *I saw Fred Blood grab his (roller) skates and do a 540 and said, "I can do that."*
> *— Mike McGill*

that has influenced all skaters trying to get air. It is still a staple of competitive skateboarding at the highest level. You are not a true vert skater until you have landed your first McTwist. Current pro skaters like Bucky Lasek have added variations such as the Kickflip McTwist and McTwist Invert. These tricks are even hard to wrap your mind around.

17. McTwist photo credits
Still photo: Mike McGill, McTwist / Photographer: Steve Badillo
Sequence: Matt Boyster, McTwist / Photographer: Steve Badillo

The McTwist is usually done on ramps and in bowls. Approach tho top of the ramp with plenty of speed. You can go straight up the transition or you can angle backside to help start the rotation. Blast your air, grabbing mute and rotating backside.

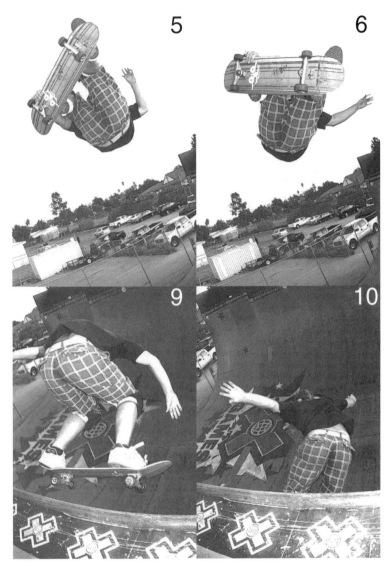

Try to over rotate the McTwist to help spin the 540. At about the 180 mark, your board should be over your head making the trick inverted. Keep the spin nice and tight and turn your head toward the transition, looking for the spot to land.

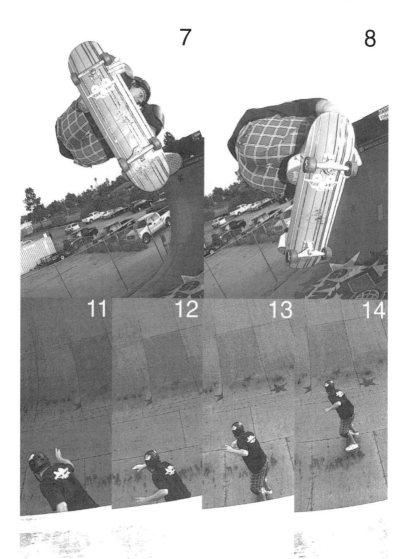

Let go of the board just before you land high on the transition. Compress as you land. Now try it 720.

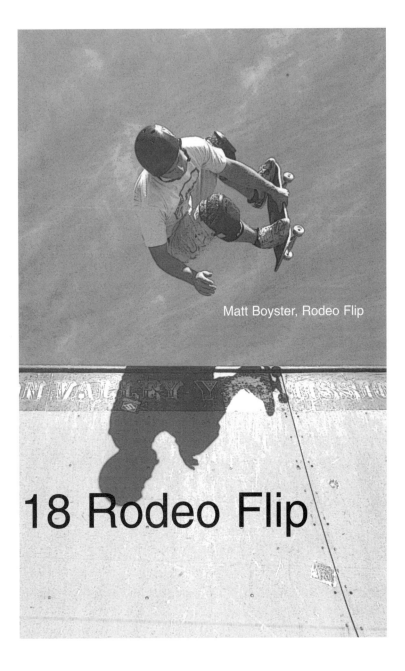

Matt Boyster, Rodeo Flip

18 Rodeo Flip

Rodeo Flip

When you see someone do a skateboard trick and the crowd cheers, that is called the "wow factor," and the Rodeo Flip has plenty of that. Every time a skater does a Rodeo Flip, the wow factor is huge.

The early form of the Rodeo Flip was called the Unit. Billy Ruff invented the Unit in the early '80s. He would do an early Grab Frontside 540 Rotation under the coping, but as he made the rotation, he would put his hand down on the transition. He put his hand down to help make the whole 540 rotation, thus basically making the Unit into a Frontside 540 Invert.

Then in 1983, Tony Hawk tried to do a Frontside 540 Air without putting his hand down on the ramp. On his own ramp, Tony tried to pull off the Rodeo Flip, but quickly realized that he needed to go higher and pull off the wall more to get the rotation down. Finally after only one day of trying, he landed it, stood up and rolled away. Tony didn't perform the Frontside 540 much until the 1990s, when the trick became more popular.

Tony's Frontside 540 Air finally got the twist that is such a big part of the Rodeo Flip from a pro street

skater named Alan Peterson. Alan first did the Rodeo Flip on launch ramps. In 1996, skaters like Andy Macdonald and Sluggo brought back the Rodeo Flip at skateparks like Woodward East, where they had a foam pit to practice the move. Then they brought it to vert ramps and performed them at the X-Games. Now the Rodeo Flip is done all the time by most vert pro skateboarders including Jake Brown, Bucky Lasek, Bob Burnquist and others.

The Rodeo Flip, like some other skateboarding tricks, has a crossover effect, especially in the snowboarding and BMX worlds. In the 1990s, snowboarding exploded in popularity, and with the added exposure, came better tricks adopted from skateboarding. The Rodeo Flip was one of those tricks. A pro snow-boarder named Daniel Franck has been doing it as one of his signature tricks since 2000.

Every time a skater does a Rodeo Flip, the wow factor is huge.

18. Rodeo Flip photo credits
Sequence: Matt Boyster, Rodeo Flip / Photographer: Steve Badillo

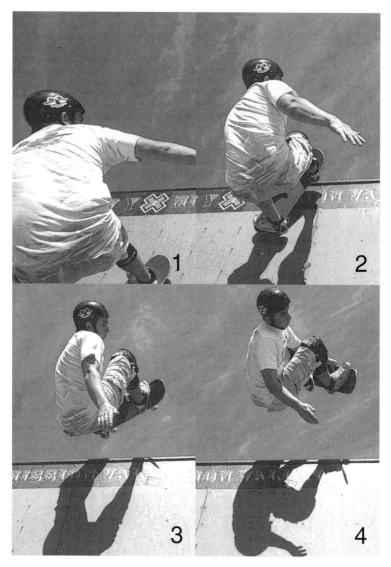

The Rodeo Flip is a Frontside 540 Air. You will need a lot of speed to help rotate the 540. Keep your feet spread on the board. Start your Frontside Air at an angle, grabbing the board with your Indy hand.

Try to huck the board frontside, turning your head and shoulders as you rotate. Look for the transition as you turn the last 180. Compress and lean toward the flatbottom. Now try it on your snowboard.

Part 5

Freestyle

When discussing freestyle skateboarding, one name stands out among all others — Rodney Mullen. Rodney has invented dozens and dozens of freestyle and streetstyle tricks. His influence in the skateboard world is undeniable and forever lasting.

But this section is about another pro freestyle skater named Primo Desiderio, who struggled to become one of the top freestyle skaters of the 1980s. The

trick he invented catapulted him to the top of the standings in contests and demos. It influenced both the freestyle skating he was doing and the street skating that came later.

19 Primoslide

Torey Pudwill, Primoslide

Primoslide
Great skaters like Rodney Mullen, Per Welinder, Kevin Harris and Pierre Andre dominated the freestyle era of the early- to mid-1980s. Those skateboarders were inventing dozens and dozens of new flat-ground tricks that would influence skaters for decades to come. One of those pro freestylers was Primo Desiderio, inventor of the Primoslide.

Primo started doing freestyle on the beaches of Venice and Huntington Beach Pier where he had crowds of a 1,000 people or more watching his fast and mesmerizing routines. That is where he met his future wife, Diane. She was watching him skate, and he offered her a ride home. A year after they met, she started skateboarding and became really good at it. They created routines together and became a couple freestyle team.

At that time in the mid-1980s, Primo was one of the top 10 sponsored freestylers in the world, but never made it to the very top, where Rodney and Per Welinder ruled. However, Primo was an extremely hard working pro skater, always trying to create new moves and routines.

Primo and Diane were skating in one of their shows when a talent scout from Sea World saw their act. The talent scout was impressed and invited Primo and Diane to perform in Sea World's new show, City Streets, which already featured BMX, break dancers and acrobats. Primo's success at Sea World and his skate sponsors made him one of the highest paid skateboarders at the time. But Primo still wasn't considered one of the top freestylers until he invented the Primoslide.

Sea World had a really slick flat ground surface. Primo was messing around one day, flipping the board to its rail and sliding a few inches. Then he tried to slide farther and farther until he was doing Primoslides 20 feet long and coming out 180. Soon he had different Primoslide variations, and that trick finally catapulted him into the rankings as one of the top five freestylers in the world. The Primoslide lives on in the performances of today's top streetstyle skateboarders like Daewon Song, Chris Haslam and Torey Pudwill.

19. Primoslide photo credits
Sequence: Torey Pudwill, Primoslide / Photographer: Steve Badillo

The Primoslide is simple, but tricky. First find some flat ground that is smooth concrete, marble or a slick surface that you can slide on. The faster you go, the longer you will slide. Line up your toes over the wheels and bolts. Have your toes hang over the

board a little bit to get good leverage. Now push down with your toes to make the board turn onto its side. As you push down, lean back onto the wheels and start sliding. Use your arms to help balance.

Slide as long as you can. Then with your front foot, push down on the nose of the board, kind of like a Nollie, and land on the bolts. Stoked! Now try it back 180 out.

Part 6

Grinds

The simple act of grinding the coping gives the skateboarder a sense of achievement that lasts as long as the grind. Skaters grind everything whether it is a ramp, pool, ledge, rail, curb or bowl. They do it to keep it flowing. They grind metal coping, pool coping, PVC coping or almost any hard surface. In the '80s they even used plastic copers on the trucks to make grinds easier.

Truck manufacturers have created different truck designs, but no matter what the design, it comes down to the truck hanger grinding on the coping. With the grind comes style and with style comes variations of the grind. This section deals with the variations of legendary grinds and the skaters that first started grinding them.

20 Feeble Grind

Josh Nelson, Feeble Grind

Feeble Grind

When Josh Nelson was growing up, his friend Sean Donnelley gave him the nickname "Feeb" (short for feeble) because he was quite skinny and often broke his limbs. But this did not stop Josh from inventing one of the most popular grinds in skateboarding. As a local skater near Del Mar, Josh and his friends put three parking blocks on top of the Del Mar reservoir ditch and sealed the blocks with epoxy. It was a double edge curb that was great for doing 50/50 Grinds, Smith Grinds, Boardslides and Slappies. Then Josh tried a Backside 50/50, but the nose did not lock into place, and he went into the Feeble Grind. Josh thought, "It's like a Smith Grind, but on top of the deck." He perfected it in the ditch that day in 1986, and his friends called it the Feeble Grind.

Josh took his Feeble Grind to the streets, curbs, mini ramps and ultimately to vert ramps and empty pools. Nowadays, Josh can be seen doing Feeble Grinds six or seven coping blocks long in the combi-bowl at Vans. After all these years the Feeble Grind has influenced all types of skateboarding.

20. Feeble Grind photo credits
Still Photo: Josh Nelson, head shot / Photographer: Steve Badillo
Sequence: Josh Nelson, Feeble Grind / Photographer: Steve Badillo

I'm stoked on how the Feeble has translated well for street skating and transition skating.
— Josh Nelson

Feeble Grinds can be done in ramps, bowls and rails. You should be able to do 50/50 Grinds before trying Feeble Grinds. Skate up to the ramp or rail with medium to fast speed (the faster the speed, the longer the grind). You should angle into the coping

like you would for a 50/50 Grind, but lift the nose up and lock the back truck into the grind while putting the nose on the top of the coping. The edge of the middle of the board should be sliding on the coping while the back truck is grinding.

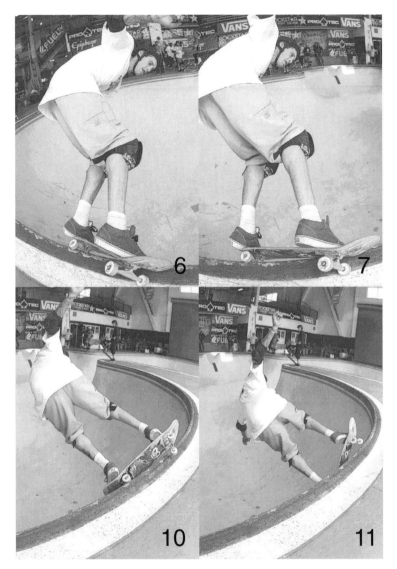

Point your front foot to help lock in the trick and lean on your heels. As you come back in, lift the nose slightly and push your back foot into a fakie position. Lean fakie and roll away.

Feeble Grind

21 Hurricane

Hurricane

Watch out — the hurricane is coming! I mean the Hurricane Grind on a skateboard. This trick is difficult to learn, but has style for days. It is a lip trick because you turn the nose frontside and lock the back truck onto the coping with the nose on the deck.

The Hurricane is believed to have been invented by the progressive and artistic pro skater Neil Blender in 1985. The first time it was revealed was in Lance Mountain's part in Powell Peralta's second video called *Future Primitive*. Neil Blender has a brief cameo in Lance's part, where Neil does a Backside Hurricane. Since then, skateboarders from all over do Hurricanes on every type of terrain.

In 1988, Tony Hawk invented the Frontside Hurricane, first on his mini ramp and then later on his vert ramp. One of the first pro skaters to do a Hurricane at the legendary skatepark, Del Mar Skate Ranch, was Tom Groholski in the keyhole bowl. The Hurricane has also translated well into street skating. Most pros use it as a staple trick on handrails, ledges and curbs.

> *Any trick where the rail is hitting the coping at the same time, your grinding is that much gnarlier.*
> — *Josh Nelson*

21. Hurricane photo credits
Sequence: Steve Badillo, Hurricane / Photographer: Gavin Badillo

Hurricanes are so fun. They can be done on ramps, rails, ledges and curbs. First learn Rock n Rolls. Ride up the transition with enough speed to do a liptrick. Lift the nose and then frontside to help the back truck lock into the Hurricane stall. The back truck should

be on the coping. Twist your head and shoulders back into the transition to rotate the nose of the board back down the ramp, just like a Rock n Roll. Stand up and try again.

22 Discolip

Ben Schroeder, Discolip

Discolip

Big Ben Schroeder is a true pioneer and originator of vertical lip tricks. If you have ever seen Ben skateboard, you know he has two speeds — fast and mach one. It is exciting to watch him skate. If you are on the course with him, watch out and get out of the way.

After winning the lip trick contest at Raging Waters in 1988, Ben took the contest money, bought a Blazer and went on tour with Reese Simpson and Ross Goodman and skated the metal ramp at Cedar Crest, Virginia. On the way to the East Coast, he stopped in Arizona and stayed the night at Allen Midget's house. The next day Allen took him to a mini ramp where Ben combined the Alley-oop 50/50 to Lipslide to Smith Grind and the Discolip was born.

At the time in the late 1980s, Ben was doing a lot of different combo lip tricks. There were no vert ramps in Los Angeles and vertical skateparks were dying off, so Ben took his frustrations out on mini ramps. He invented tricks like Tailslide, Tailslide Reverts, Lien to Tail Reverts, Lipslide Reverts, Alley-oop Nose Grinds, Nose Bone Frontside Grinds (Salad Grinds), Backside Disaster to Frontside Smith, Tail Drop Reverts and many others.

Skate magazines called this type of skating "switch." The idea of switch skating had arrived and was embraced by the street skating scene in particular.

> *You are doing a combination of things on the lip, like disco dancing, so I'm calling it (sarcastically) Discolip.*
> *— Ben Schroeder*

22. Discolip photo credits
Still Photo: Ben Schroeder, Discolip / Photographer: Steve Badillo
Sequence: Ben Schroeder, Discolip / Photographer: Steve Badillo

The Discolip is a combo lip trick. Broken down, it is a Backside Alley-oop 50/50 to Lipslide to Smith Grind. You may want to learn 50/50 Grinds, Lipslides and Smith Grinds before trying this trick. You need to be going as fast as you can to make it work. Approach

the coping at an angle to start the Alley-oop 50/50. Lift the nose up to help lock into the 50/50. Lean on the heel side while grinding and dip your head into the transition so you stay balanced and don't fly off the lip. While in the Alley-oop 50/50 Grind, rotate the

nose under the coping so it becomes a Lipslide.
Then while you are Lipsliding, crank the back truck
into a Smith Grind. Lean into the transition and skate
away. Big Ben would be proud.

23 Suski Grind

Suski Grind

Once in a while a skater has so much style while doing a trick that kids start calling the trick by the skater's name. That is the case with the Suski Grind.

Aaron Suski started doing Backside 5-0 Grinds while sliding on the tail in the early 1990s. His style was so smooth and the skateboard so tweaked out while doing the grind, that other skaters called that type of 5-0 a Suski Grind.

Aaron never claimed to be the first skater to do the Suski Grind and is amazed that people still call it that. The first time Aaron got coverage of the trick was on an Emerica tour in Australia. He did the Suski Grind on a ledge off a double set of stairs. His friends were calling it a Sidewinder, but after more and more coverage, kids started calling it the Suski Grind (even though it is not clear who really named the trick).

Aaron was not the first to do the grind. I remember watching Dogtown and Alva Posse skaters do the same grind around 1988 in Venice on the boardwalk. I skated with guys like Chris Cook, John Thomas and Jeff Hartsel.

They were doing backside 5-0 Grinds and sliding their tails on curbs and small ledges. Now when you say Suski Grind, it basically describes how the 5-0 Grind is being done. Try it frontside and backside.

His style was so smooth and the skateboard so tweaked out while doing the grind that other skaters called that type of 5-0 a Suski Grind.

23. Suski Grind photo credits
Sequence: Steve Badillo, Suski Grind / Photographer: Gavin Badillo

Suski Grinds are done on ledges, rails and curbs. The Suski Grind is basically a tweaked out Backside 5-0 Grind while sliding on the tail. Your speed will vary depending on the obstacle you are skating. The faster you go, the longer the grind. Ollie up to the lip

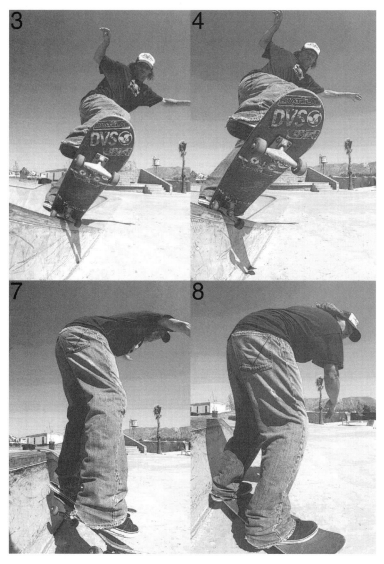

of the ledge or rail and into a Backside 5-0 Grind, but tweak the nose toward the flatbottom or backside. While grinding, the tail should also be sliding on the ledge. Hold the grind as long as you can. Then turn the nose off the ledge and land on the bolts.

Suski Grind

24 Barley Grind

Anthony Janow, Barley Grind

Barley Grind

Skateboard videos are a big part of professional skateboarding. These videos can inspire and change the lives of young skaters. Sometimes pro skaters use their video part to introduce new tricks or terrain to the skateboard world. They are fun to watch and make you want to get up and skate.

When Donny Barley was an amateur for Toy Machine in 1995, he was staying with Ed Templeton, and they skated Huntington Skatepark alot. Donny would watch Ed do crazy grinds on the flatbar, like Front Feebles. So Donny started doing Smith and Feeble variations. Then while hanging with Tom Penny and Chad Muska, Donny recalls trying to keep up with those guys and trying new tricks. Finally at Huntington Skatepark, Donny landed his first Barley Grind.

Donny Barley used his video part in Toy Machine's *Welcome To Hell* in 1996 to introduce the Barley Grind to skaters everywhere. In his video part, Donny does the Barley Grind both ways — on handrails, back to back. The Barley Grind is a Switch Frontside 180 Ollie into a Smith Grind, and it is also a Frontside 180 Ollie into a Switch Smith Grind. It is a trick that can be done two ways. This is partly why the Barley Grind is legendary. When Donny Barley first did these grinds in the *Welcome To Hell* video, it blew people's minds. It showed that there were still new grinds to be invented and also that the use of combinations of tricks together can create new moves.

> *To figure it out, I manipulated the board with different Smith variations and then realized how to land it.*
> — Donny Barley

What influenced Donny to try this grind was Mark Gonzales in the *Blind Video Days* film — where Gonz was doing all kinds of weird tricks and grinds. After watching Mark's part, Donny went out to learn the grind both ways, switch and regular. Donny's favorite way to do the Barley Grind is Frontside 180 to Switch Smith.

Donny does not know if he was truly the first one to do this grind, but he is stoked that his name is linked to the trick. Michael Burnett, who is a famous skate photographer, is credited with actually naming it the Barley Grind.

24. Barley Grind photo credits
Sequence: Anthony Janow, Barley Grind / Photographer: Steve Badillo

Start out rolling medium speed toward a ledge, handrail or flatbar. You will be rolling switch, placing your feet in the Switch Ollie position. Snap your Ollie and start rotating frontside 180. Aim for the back truck to lock into the Smith Grind. To allow the nose

to stay down, straighten your front leg. Grind through the Smith by leaning forward and lifting the nose slightly to level out. Land it and roll away. Try it Frontside 180 Ollie into Switch Smith Grind.

Barley Grind

Part 7

Street

Street skating in itself is freedom. Being able to go outside your house and explore the natural terrain is what attracts people to street skating. Bombing hills with your friends, finding a ditch, kickflipping a set of stairs, grinding a nice painted red curb or tailsliding a ledge — these are the activities the street skater searches for. The legendary street skaters of this last section are monumentally influential and have left a lasting impression on the skateboard world.

25 Natas Spin

Natas Spin

Natas Kaupas grew up in Santa Monica near the area known as Dogtown. He is considered one of the first 100 percent pure street skateboarders. Preferring not to skate in skateparks or ride ramps, he revolutionized street skating with his high Ollie and imaginative creation of tricks in the streets.

After receiving a Santa Monica Airlines skateboard as a first place prize in a surf contest, Natas used the streets to focus his skateboarding skills. Natas did lots of different curb tricks, wallrides and flat ground tricks using his naturally high Ollie to progress street skating. From this progression, he took the Kickflip to the streets — doing Kickflips off curbs, over gaps and on banks.

He also was one of the first to do Boardslides on handrails. After an initial unsuccessful attempt in a contest in 1986, Natas landed the first Boardslide on a handrail along with legendary skater Mark Gonzales.

In 1989, Santa Cruz Skateboards released *Streets on Fire* where Natas performed the Natas Spin on a fire hydrant. He Ollied on top of a fire hydrant and did a 720 Degree Frontside Spin and landed it, shocking skaters everywhere. A new shoe company called Etnies emerged around that time and asked Natas to endorse

a signature shoe model, something that was a new concept for skateboard shoe companies. Natas himself contributed to the shoe's design. Pro skater signature shoes have been flooding the market ever since. The Natas Spin was included as a special trick in Activision's *Tony Hawk Underground 2* video game.

Natas and other street pro skaters from the late 1980s truly transformed the skate industry from vert transition skating to street style skating. Since impacting the skateboard world as a pro rider, Natas has worked as a graphic designer for Quiksilver and Element skateboards. The Natas Spin is very difficult and is not done by very many skaters. It is considered a legendary trick for its creativity and use of natural terrain.

The Natas Spin is usually done on fire hydrants, small poles or stumps. They can be done frontside or backside from a 360 or 720 Spin. Skate up to the fire hydrant with slow speed. Snap your Ollie and start rotating frontside.

Land on the hydrant in the middle of your board and continue to spin frontside. Use your head and shoulders to help rotate the board. After you complete the 360 or 720 Spin, swing the nose of the board off and roll away.

Natas took the terrain and reshuffled it, opening the eyes of skateboard companies to where skateboarding was heading.
— Skip Engblom

25. Natas Spin photo credits
Still Photo: Natas drawing by Zach Wagner / Photographer: Zach Wagner
Sequence: Steve Badillo, Natas Spin / Photographer: Gavin Badillo

26 Hardflip

Mike Mo Capaldi, Hardflip

> *This trick is tough, no doubt, but the skater who is able to perfect his/her Hardflip will command much respect at the skatepark.*

Hardflip
Hard is the perfect adjective to describe this difficult flip trick. The Hardflip looks so good when a skater does it right. There are a couple of ways to do the Hardflip, either horizontally or vertically through the legs. Both ways are hard, but vertically through the legs is gnarly.

Many people credit Rodney Mullen with the Hardflip's invention, but it was first introduced to the skateboard world by legendary skateboarder Daewon Song in the 1992 World Industries skate video, *Love Child*. Daewon does a slow motion version of the move for his final trick over a dirt gap. Like so many legendary tricks, it is not known who the first skater to actually do it is.

Other skateboarders popularized the trick, like Chet Thomas, Kareem Campbell and Kris Markovich. Chad "the Muska" Muska does one of the best Hardflips in the business. He does it through his legs with a giant Ollie.

The Hardflip can be done down stairs, on banks, in ramps, over gaps or just about anywhere. Depending on where you do it, your speed will vary. You should learn Frontside Flips and Shove Its before trying Hardflips. Get into the Kickflip position just on your toes.

26. Hardflip
Sequence: Mike Mo Capaldi, Hardflip / Photographer: Steve Badillo

Snap your Frontside Flip, but do not rotate your body. Keep your knees bent and above your board so that it can fully flip around 180 underneath you. Catch the board on the bolts and stomp your landing. Mo knows Hardflips.

27 Ghetto Bird

Brandon Read, Ghetto Bird

Ghetto Bird

One legendary street skater from the 1990s who had a huge influence on streetstyle was Kareem Campbell. Kareem turned pro in 1992 when street skating was the wave that was carrying skateboarding. As vert skating started to die off, skaters like Kareem were able to put streetstyle to the forefront of skateboarding with technical tricks like the Ghetto Bird.

Kareem had both style and switch stance in his skateboarding skills. Although Kareem is credited with inventing the Ghetto Bird (he named the trick), he might not have actually been the first skater to do it. But the Ghetto Bird became his signature move along with the Nollie Ghetto Bird. When other skaters were doing their tricks, Kareem was doing them switch. In the 1993 World Industries video, *New World Order,* Kareem shows how to do it switch stance and how to go big.

The Ghetto Bird is also featured as a special move in the Tony Hawk video game series. The move is a difficult trick to land, and only very skilled street skateboarders can do it.

The Ghetto Bird is a combo flip trick. It combines the Hardflip and a Backside 180. You should first learn Hardflips and Backside 180 Ollies. This trick can be done on flat ground, down stairs and over gaps. Start skating with slow to medium speed, depending on

the obstacle you are skating. Your feet should be in the Hardflip position. Snap your Ollie with your front foot, flicking the board into a Frontside Flip Shove It. While in the air, start rotating your body backside 180.

In the 1993 World Industries video, New World Order, Kareem shows how to do it switch stance and how to go big.

Try to catch the board in the air to help rotate the 180 part. Land on the bolts and lean fakie. Good luck with this one.

28
Laser
Flip

Kristos Andrews, Laser Flip

Laser Flip

The Laser Flip is one of the most technical flip tricks to perform. It is a 360 Heelflip and is a lot harder then it sounds. Getting the board to rotate 360 while in the Heelflip is difficult because it is awkward kicking your feet out to make the flip and land back on the board.

Rodney Mullen is given credit for inventing the trick, but it did not become popular until the mid-1990s through pro street skaters like Ronnie Creager and Kerry Getz. Chris Haslam also does Laser Flips with style, like it was no problem. In the Es game of SKATE, pro skaters use the Laser Flip competitively against other pro skaters. Chris Haslam did it against Eric Koston, and Eric received a letter. Besides in video parts and the game of SKATE, you won't see many Laser Flips. When you see someone do the trick, take note because they are rare sightings.

> *When you see someone do the trick, take note because they are rare sightings.*

28. Laser Flip photo credits
Sequence: Kristos Andrews, Laser Flip / Photographer: Steve Badillo

Laser Flips are straight up difficult. They can be done on flat ground, down stairs and over gaps. First learn Heelflips and get them wired. Set up in the Heelflip position, with your front foot toes over the edge of the board and your back foot in the Frontside Shove

It position. If you are trying it on flat ground, your speed is slow. Your speed should be medium to fast if going down stairs. Snap your Ollie and kick out your Heelflip using your front foot to rotate the board Frontside 360 Heelflip.

7
8
11
12

At the same time, use your back foot to help the board spin around frontside 360. Get your knees bent and up over the board so the board can spin all the way around. Catch the board on the bolts and land it.

13   14

29 Pole Jam

Pole Jam

The Pole Jam may not be a legendary trick, but it is definitely super fun and exciting. The Pole Jam is a street trick using an Ollie and grinding up any bent pole.

It is not known who was the first to do it, but the Pole Jam appeared in street skating in the early 1990s. When skateparks closed down due to insurance hysteria, skaters brought their boards to the streets and used the terrain to keep the sport alive. Skaters like Mark Gonzales, Jason Lee, Guy Mariano and others popularized Pole Jams. The pole was an obstacle that could be found by skaters anywhere, and its lure was insatiable.

Pole Jam variations are created and performed by many different skaters. Daewon Song does an array of different Pole Jams in the skate film, *Cheese and Crackers*. Daewon does a Pole Jam Rock to Fakie from a halfpipe that is particularly impressive. Now when skateparks or street contests are built, many have Pole Jams constructed into them. Find yourself a bent pole and try it out.

Chapter 29

Pole Jams are done on bent poles. Find a bent or slanted pole and skate up to it with enough speed to grind up. You will snap an Ollie just before you hit the pole. Keep your Ollie nice and straight. Lift the nose as your back truck starts grinding the pole.

Lean forward and flatten out your board with your front foot while landing. Now try it switch.

Bibliography

Adrenalinsports.nl, http://www.adrenalinsports.nl/skate/item/lance-mountain-stopt-met-the-firm, 2009

Allexperts.com, http://en.allexperts.com/e/g/gr/grinds_(skateboarding).htm, 2009

Antics, http://www.uptheantics.com/features/article/lance_mountain, 2009

Cliver, Sean. Disposable. Thornhill, Ontario Canada: Concrete Wave Editions, 2004

Concrete Disciples,
http://www.concretedisciples.com/skate_photos/details.php?image_id=603, 2009

Deaf Skateboards, http://www.deafskateboards.com/squad/node/14, 2009
Economicexpert.com, http://www.economicexpert.com/a/Skateboarding:tricks.htm, 2009

Exhibit Gallery, http://www.exhibitagallery.com/index.php?aid=42-4, 2009

Floridaskater.com,
http://www.floridaskater.com/floridaskater%20bruce%20walker%20profile.htm, 2009

Freebase, http://www.freebase.com/view/en/hardflip, 2009

Funtrivia.com, http://www.funtrivia.com/en/subtopics/Snowboard-Tricks-184483.html, 2009

Gassigns.org, http://www.gassigns.org/phil66.htm, 2009

Hawk, Tony. Hawk. New York, New York: Regan Books, 2001

Mullen, Rodney. The Mutt. New York, New York: Regan Books, 2004

Oeus.com, http://www.odeus.com/blog/vintage-skateboard-advertisements/, 2009

Olliewood.ogr, http://www.olliewood.org/about.html, 2009

Skateboard-city.com, http://www.skateboard-city.com/messageboard/archive/index.php/t-61237.html, 2009

Skateboarder 2.0, http://tricks.skateboarder2.com/aerials.htm, 2009

Skateboarder 2.0, http://tricks.skateboarder2.com/freestyle.htm, 2009

Skateboarder 2.0, http://tricks.skateboarder2.com/other-tricks.htm, 2009

Skatekings.com, http://sk8kings.com/new/primo_d.htm, 2009

Sports.jrank.org, http://sports.jrank.org/pages/3700/Peters-Duane-Invented-

Skateboarding-Tricks.html, 2009

steviecaballero.blogspot.com, http://steviecaballero.blogspot.com/2009/10/fakie-360-ollie-invented-29-years-ago.html, 2009

The Free Library, http://www.thefreelibrary.com/Five+great+inverts+with+Tony+Hank.-a0196381553, 2009

Thrasher Magazine, November 1983,
http://www.thrashermagazine.com/index.php?option=com_content&task=view&id=1938&Itemid=38, 2009

Today's Pentecostal Evangel, http://www.ag.org/pentecostal-evangel/Articles2003/4645_noonan.cfm, 2009

Wikipedia, http://en.wikipedia.org/wiki/Aerials_(skateboarding)#Judo_Air, 2009

Wikipedia, http://en.wikipedia.org/wiki/Bob_Burnquist, 2009

Wikipedia, http://en.wikipedia.org/wiki/Grinds_(skateboarding), 2009

Wikipedia, http://en.wikipedia.org/wiki/Lip_tricks, 2009

Zolum.com, http://www.zolum.com/xsports/skate/73/skateboarding-trick-guide, 2009

Resources

In alphabetical order we have a healthy dose of info about skateboarding as it relates to:

Books
Camps
Magazines
Museums
Organizations
Shops
Skateparks
Skatepark Designers
Television
Videos
Web Sites

For a quick fix go to skateboarding.com
This is an informative (but not the only) portal into the skateboarding galaxy. For face-to-face, find a real skateboard shop and talk to skaters.

Books

Books discovered on Amazon.com and Barnesandnoble.com

Baccigaluppi, John. Declaration of Independents. San Francisco, California: Chronicle Books, 2001.

Bermudez, Ben. Skate! The Mongo's Guide to Skateboarding. New York, New York: Cheapskate Press, 2001.

Borden, Ian. Skateboarding, Space and the City. New York, New York: Berg, 2001.

Brooke, Michael. The Concrete Wave: The History of Skateboarding. Toronto, Ontario: Warwick Publishing, 1999.

Burke, L.M. Skateboarding! Surf the Pavement. New York, New York: Rosen Publishing Group, Inc., 1999.

Cliver, Sean. Disposable: A History of Skateboarding Art

Davis, James. Skateboard Roadmap. England: Carlton Books Limited, 1999.

Gould, Marilyn. Skateboarding. Mankato, Minnesota: Capstone Press, 1991.

Gutman, Bill. Skateboarding: To the Extreme. New York, New York: Tom Doherty Associates, Inc., 1997.

Hardwicke, Catherine. Lords of Dogtown. Thornhill, Ontario, Canada: Concrete Wave Editions, 2005.

Hawk, Tony. Occupation: Skateboarder. New York, New York: Regan Books 2001.

Mullen, Rodney. The Mutt: How to Skateboard and not Kill Yourself. New York, New York: Regan Books 2004.

Powell, Ben. Extreme Sports: Skateboarding. Hauppauge, New York: Barron's Educational Series, Inc., 1999.

Riggins, Edward. Ramp Plans. San Francisco, California: High Speed Productions, 2000.

Ryan, Pat. Extreme Skateboarding, Mankato, Minnesota: Capstone Press, 1998.

Shoemaker, Joel. Skateboarding Streetstyle, Mankato, Minnesota: Capstone Press

Thornhill, Ontario: Concrete Wave Editions 2004.

Thrasher. Insane Terrain. New York, New York: Universe Publishing, 2001.

Camps

IPS
School of Skate
P.O. Box 1530
Hood River, OR 97031
School_of_skate@sk8ips.com

Lake Owen
HC 60 Box 60
Cable, WI 54821
715-798-3785

Magdalena Ecke Family YMCA
200 Saxony Road
Encinitas, CA 92023-0907
760-942-9622

Mission Valley YMCA
5505 Friars Road
San Diego, CA 92110
619-298-3576

SkateLab
Steve Badillo Skate Camp
4226 Valley Fair St.
Simi Valley, CA 93063
805-578-0040
skatelab.com

Snow Valley
PO Box 2337
Running Springs, CA 92382
909-867-2751

Visalia YMCA
Sequoia Lake, California
211 West Tulare Avenue
Visalia, CA 93277
559-627-0700

Woodward Camp
PO Box 93
132 Sports Camp Drive
Woodward, PA 16882
814-349-5633

Woodward Lake Owen
46445 Krafts Point Road
Cable, WI 54821
715-798-3785

Woodward West
28400 Stallion Springs Road
Tehachapi, CA 93561
661-882-7900

Young Life Skate Camp
Hope, British Columbia, Canada
604-807-3718

Magazines

Juice
319 Ocean Front Walk #1
Venice, CA 90291
310-399-5336
www.juicemagazine.com
info@juicemagazine.com

Skateboarder
Surfer Publications
PO Box 1028
Dana Point, CA 92629
www.skateboardermag.com

Thrasher
High Speed Productions
1303 Underwood Avenue

San Francisco, CA 94124
415-822-3083
www.thrashermagazine.com

Transworld Skateboarding
353 Airport Road
Oceanside, CA 92054
760-722-7777
www.skateboarding.com

Museums

Board Gallery
Newport Beach, CA

Huntington Beach International Skate
and Surf Museum
411 Olive St.
Huntington Beach, CA
714-960-3483

SkateLab
4226 Valley Fair St.
Simi Valley, CA 93063
805-578-0040
www.skatelab.com

Skatopia
34961 Hutton Rd.
Rutland, OH 45775
740-742-1110

Organizations

Action Sports Retailer
Organizer of the Action Sports Retailer
Trade Expos
949-376-8144
asrbiz.com

C.A.S.L. and P.S.L.
California Amateur Skateboard League
Professional Skateboard League
Amateur and professional contest
organizer
909-883-6176
Fax 909-883-8036

Extreme Downhill International
1666 Garnet Ave. #308
San Diego, CA 92109
619-272-3095

Grind For Life
Helping People With Cancer
www.grindforlife.org

International Association of
Skateboard Companies
P.O. Box 37
Santa Barbara, CA 93116

805-683-5676
iascsk8@aol.com
skateboardiasc.org

International Network for Flatland
Freestyle Skateboarding
Abbedissavagen 15
746 95 Balsta, Sweden

KC Projects
Canadian amateur contest organizer
514-806-7838
kc_projects@aol.com
5148067838@fido.ca

National Amateur Skateboard
Championships
Damn Am Series
National amateur contest organizer
813-621-6793
skateparkoftampa.com
nascseries.com

N.H.S.S.A.
National High School Skateboard
Association
www.sk8nhssa.com
jeff@sk8nhssa.com
jeffreystern@roadrunner.com
805-990-4209

National Skateboarders Association of
Australia (NSAA)
Amateur and professional contest
organizer
61-2-9878-3876
skateboard.asn.au

The Next Cup
Southern California amateur contest
organizer
858-874-4970 Ext. 114 or 129
www.thenextcup.com

Skateboarding Association of America
Amateur contest organizer
727-523-0875
www.skateboardassn.org

Skatepark Association of the USA
(SPAUSA)
Resource for skatepark planning /
operating
310-823-9228
www.spausa.org

Supergirl
www.beasupergirl.com

Southwest Sizzler
Southwestern amateur contest organizer
918-638-6492

Surf Expo
East Coast trade show
800-947-SURF
www.surfexpo.com

United Skateboarding Association
(USA)
Skate event organizer and action sport
marketing / promotions
732-432-5400 Ext. 2168 and 2169
www.unitedskate.com

Vans Shoes
Organizer of the Triple Crown skate
events
562-565-8267
www.vans.com

World Cup Skateboarding
Organizer of some of skating's largest
events
530-888-0296
Danielle@wcsk8.com
www.wcsk8.com

Zeal Skateboarding Association
Southern California amateur contest
organizer
909-265-3420
www.zealsk8.com

Shops And Companies

Fountain of Youth
60 Eddy St.
Providence, RI 02903
www.foy-skateshop.com
www.grandburo.com

IPS Skateboards
IPS Skate & Snow Shop
13 Oak Street
Hood River, OR 97031
541-386-6466
www.sk8ips.com
wally@sk8ips.com
skateshop@sk8ips.com

Momentum Surf Company
607 W. Channel Island Blvd.
Port Hueneme, CA 93041
805-985-4929
www.momentumsurfco.com

Old Man Army Skateboards
2053 E Alameda Dr.
Tempe, AZ 85282
www.oldmanarmy.com

Skateboarding.com

Skateboards.org

SkateLab
4226 Valley Fair St.
Simi Valley, CA 93063
805-578-0040
www.skatelab.com

SteadHam Skate Ind.
www.stevesteadham.com
myspace.com/stevesteadham
stevesteadham@hotmail.com
ssteadham@gmail.com
702-416-8331

Tailtap
PO Box 1895
Carlsbad, CA 92018
www.tailtap.com

Skateparks

Clairmont Skatepark
3401 Clairmont Dr.
San Diego, CA

Culver City Skateboard Park
Jefferson Blvd. and Duquesne Ave.
Culver City, CA

Duarte Skatepark
1401 Central Ave.
Duarte, CA

Fillmore Skatepark
C Street
Fillmore, CA

Oxnard Skatepark
3250 South Rose Avenue
Oxnard, CA

San Pedro Skatepark
Channel St.
San Pedro, CA

Santa Monica The Cove Skatepark
14th St.
Santa Monica, CA

SkateLab
4226 Valley Fair St.
Simi Valley, CA 93063
805-578-0040

www.skatelab.com

Upland Skatepark

Vans The Block
20 City Blvd. West
Orange, CA

Skatepark Designers

Airspeed Skateparks LLC
2006 Highway 101 #154
Florence, OR 97439
503-791-4674
airspeed@airspeedskateparks.com
www.airspeedskateparks.com

CA Skateparks, Design / Build and
General Contracting
273 North Benson Avenue
Upland, CA 91786
562-208-4646
www.skatedesign.com

Dreamland Skateparks, LLC
960 SE Hwy 101
PMB 384
Lincoln City, OR 97367-2622
(503) 577-9277
www.dreamlandskateparks.com

Grindline Inc.
4619 14th Ave SW
Seattle, WA 98106
(206) 932-6414
www.grindline.com

John Woodstock Designs
561-743-5963
johnwoodstock@msn.com
www.woodstockskateparks.com

Freshpark / Radius 8, Inc.
5900 Hollis Street, Suite S
Emeryville, CA 94608-2008
800-490-2709
info@freshpark.com
www.freshpark.com

Ramptech
www.ramptech.com

RCMC Custom Cement Skateparks
www.rcmcsk8parks.com

Spectrum Skatepark Creations, Ltd.
M/A 2856 Clifftop Lane
Whistler, B.C.
V0N 1B2 Canada
250-238-0140
design@spectrum-sk8.com

www.spectrum-sk8.com

Team Pain
864 Gazelle Trail
Winter Springs, FL 32708
407-695-8215
tim@teampain.com
www.teampain.com

Professional Skateboarding Events

All Girl Skate Jam
www.myspace.com (Search for All Girl
Skate Jam)

Etnies Goofy Vs. Regular
gvr.etniesskate.com

Gravity Games H2O
Gravitygamesh20.com

Maloof Money Cup
maloofmoneycup.com

Mountain Dew Tour
www.astdewtour.com

Tony Hawk's Boom Boom Huck Jam
www.boomboomhuckjam.com

Warped Tour
www.vans.com/vans/events

Vans Triple Crown of Skateboarding
www.vans.com/vans/events

X Games
Expn.go.com/expn

Web Sites

www.exploratorium.edu/skateboarding
Glossary, scientific explanations and
equipment for skating.

www.interlog.com/~mbrooke/skategee
zer.html
International Longboarder magazine.

www.ncdsa.com
Northern California Downhill
Skateboarding Association.

www.skateboard.com
Chat and messages.

www.skateboarding.com
Every skater's site by Transworld
Skateboarding magazine.

www.skateboards.org

Find parks, shops and companies
here.

www.skatelab.com
One of Los Angeles area's largest
indoor parks and world's largest skateboard museum.

www.smithgrind.com
Skate news wire.

www.switchmagazine.com
Switch Skateboarding Magazine

www.thrashermagazine.com
A comprehensive site by Thrasher
magazine.

www.tailtap.com
Your direct source for hard to find
books and magazines.

More Web Sites

360flip.com
answers.com
ben10schroeder.com
blacklabelskates.com
blackplaguewheels.com
blitzdistribution.com
bluetileobsession.com
board-crazy.co.uk
concretedisciple.com
crailtap.com
dvsskate.com
dwindle.com
ehow.com
eightequalsd.com
everything2.com
experiencefestival.com
floridaskater.com
forheavenskate.com
glidemagazine.com
grindforlife.org
halfpintskateboards.com
how2skate.com
imdb.com
juicemagazine.com
juicemagazine.com
kellylynn.com
kidzworld.com
lancemountain.com
mayaskates.com
mcgillsskateshop.com
myspace.com
oldmanarmy.com
ollieair.com
podiumdist.com
premise.tv
rainbowskateparks.com
rodneymullen.net

ruggedelegantliving.com
scholastic.com
secretsofsuccess.com
sk8ips.com
sk8kings.com
sk8trip.com
skateamerica.com
skateboarddirectory.com
skateboarder2.com
skatelab.com
skatelegends.com
skatepunk.net
smallbeating.com
socalskateparks.com
stevebadillo@roadrunner.com
tailtap.com
thinkquest.org
tonyhawk.com
twsbiz.com
ty-page.com
wikihow.com
wikipedia.org
www.stevebadillo.net
youtube.com

Videos / Instructional

411 Video Productions. The First Step.

411 Video Productions. The Next Step.

Hawk, Tony. Tony Hawk's Trick Tips
Volume I: Skateboarding Basics. 900
Films, 2001.

Hawk, Tony. Tony Hawk's Trick Tips
Volume II: Essentials of Street. 900
Films, 2001.

Thrasher Magazine. How to
Skateboard. San Francisco, California:
High Speed Productions, Inc., 1995.

Thrasher Magazine. How to
Skateboard Better. San Francisco,
California: High Speed Productions,
Inc., 1997.

Transworld Skateboarding. Starting
Point. Oceanside, California, 1997.

Transworld Skateboarding. Trick Tips
with Wily Santos. Oceanside,
California, 1998.

Transworld Skateboarding. Starting
Point Number Two. Oceanside,
California, 1999.

Steve's Sponsors

Santa Monica Airlines Skateboards
3435 Ocean Park Blvd. #107/151
Santa Monica, CA 90405
www.smaskateboards.com

Skatelab
4226 Valley Fair St.
Simi Valley, CA 93063
805-578-0040
www.skatelab.com

DVS Shoe Company
955 Francisco Street
Torrance, CA 90502
www.dvsshoes.com
www.dvsskate.com

Black Plague Wheels
www.blackplaguewheels.com

Index

Tricks

Photo Credits pages 188, 200, 206, 208-215

Still Photo: Tony Hawk, Caballerial
Photographer: Steve Badillo

Still Photo: Eddie Hadvina, Smith Grind
Photographer: Steve Badillo

Still Photo: Bennet Harada, Frontside air
Photographer: Steve Badillo

Still Photo: Melissa O'Grady, Frontside Grind
Photographer Steve Badillo

Still Photo: Steve Badillo, Frontside Rock n Roll
Photographer: Mark Partain

Still Photo: Rex Heery, Acid Drop
Photographer: Steve Badillo

Still Photo: Christian Hosoi, Layback Grind
Photographer: Becca Badillo

Still Photo: Steve Badillo, Lipslide
Photographer: Gavin Badillo

Still Photo: Steve Caballero, Frontside Grind
Photographer: Steve Badillo

Still Photo: Overhead view of combi bowl
Photographer: Steve Badillo

Still Photo: Benji Galloway, Frontside Rock n Roll
Photographer: Steve Badillo

Still Photo: Josh Borden, McTwist
Photographer: Steve Badillo

Still Photo: Steve Badillo, Fakie
Photographer: Gavin Badillo

Still Photo: Steve Badillo, Frontside Air
Photographer: Gavin Badillo

Still Photo: Steve Badillo, Tail Grab
Photographer: Gavin Badillo

Still Photo: David Loy, Hurricane
Photographer: Steve Badillo

Still Photo: Torey Pudwill, Switch Frontside Flip
Photographer: Steve Badillo

Still Photo: Bob Burnquist, Switch Stalefish
Photographer: Steve Badillo

Still Photo: Torey Pudwill, Frontside Feeble
Photographer: Steve Badillo

Still Photo: Zander Gabriel, Feeble Grind
Photographer: Steve Badillo

Still Photo: Legendary Skaters
Photographer: Steve Badillo

Still Photo: Duane Peters, Layback Roll Out
Photographer: Steve Badillo

Still Photo: Steve Caballero, Frontside Invert
Photographer: Steve Badillo

Still Photo: Lance Mountain, Feeble Grind
Photographer: Steve Badillo

Still Photo: Lance Mountain, Frontside Invert
Photographer: Steve Badillo

Still Photo: Mike Mo Capaldi, Barley Grind
Photographer: Steve Badillo

Still Photo: Gavin Badillo, Manual
Photographer: Steve Badillo

Still Photo: Steve Badillo, Frontside Air
Photographer: Ozzie Ausband

Still Photo: Lance Mountain, Judo Air
Photographer: Steve Badillo

Still Photo: Andrew Murray, Sweeper
Photographer: Donna Murray

Still Photo: Lizzie Armanto
Photographer: Steve Badillo

211

stevebadillo.net

Steve Badillo has co-authored four top selling skateboarding guides including *Skateboarder's Start-Up, Skateboarding: New Levels, Skateboarding: Book of Tricks and Skateboarding: Legendary Tricks.* He is a sponsored pro skater, runs the SkateLab Skate Camp near Los Angeles, and has worked as a stunt double and actor in numerous commercials and films featuring skateboarding including *Lords of Dogtown.* Steve is the head judge for the National High School Skateboard Association, a nationwide skateboarding program for high schools.

TRACKS

Our sport instructional guides are best-sellers because each book contains hundreds of images, is packed with expert advice and retails at a great price. No one else comes close.

Start-Up Sports® tackles the hottest sports. Forthright. Simple.
— Library Journal

trackspublishing.com